A trio of European experts in psychology, theology and apologetics offer a fascinating and thoroughly biblical response, not just to the current Covid crisis, but to every crisis. The authors confront the raw reality of suffering with a vibrant resurrection hope.

Jeremy McQuoid

Teaching Pastor at Deeside Christian Fellowship
Chair of Council, Keswick Ministries

When a storm such as this pandemic is raging, it is vital to drop the strong anchor of Christian hope into the bedrock of God's Word, God's promises and God's proven faithfulness. This short book does exactly that. And when many false assumptions and apocalyptic theories swirl around, it is vital to be assured of what the Bible does (and doesn't) teach about evil and suffering. This book does that too. Simple but solidly biblical, tackling tough issues in a very readable way – I strongly commend it.

Chris Wright

Langham Partnership
Author of *The God I Don't Understand*

Living in such turbulent times, people are inevitably asking the question: 'Where can I find hope and security in the midst of suffering and uncertainty?' This book will help many as it provides satisfying answers and great comfort, rooted in the promises of God in Scripture.

Lindsay Brown

Former General Secretary of IFES
International Director, Lausanne Movement

The
ONLY
COMFORT
in
LIFE
and
DEATH

Faith and Hope in the Pandemic

Jonathan Lamb
Giacomo Carlo Di Gaetano
Pablo Martinez

CHRISTIAN
FOCUS

Scripture, unless otherwise marked, is taken from the *Holy Bible, New International Version®*. NIV®. Copyright ©1973, 1978, 1984, 2011 by International Bible Society. Used by permission of Zondervan. All rights reserved.

Scripture quotations marked 'ESV' are from *The Holy Bible, English Standard Version*, copyright © 2001 by Crossway Bibles, a publishing ministry of Good news Publishers. Used by permission. All rights reserved. ESV Text Edition: 2011.

Scripture quotations marked 'NKJV' are taken from the *New King James Version*. Copyright © 1982 by Thomas Nelson, Inc. Used by permission. All rights reserved.

Copyright © Jonathan Lamb, Pablo Martinez
& Giacomo Carlo Di Gaetano 2020

The authors have waived royalty payments in favour of *Blythswood Care*, a Christian charity which supports the vulnerable, including those impacted by Covid-19.

paperback ISBN 978-1-5271-0635-2
epub ISBN 978-1-5271-0643-7
mobi ISBN 978-1-5271-0644-4

Published in 2020
by
Christian Focus Publications Ltd,
Geanies House, Fearn, Ross-shire
IV20 1TW, Scotland
www.christianfocus.com

Cover design by Daniel Van Straaten
Printed and bound by Bell & Bain, Glasgow

CONTENTS

Italian edition: *L'unico conforto nella vita e nella morte: credere e sperare nella pandemia*, published by Edizioni GBU. Go to: https://edizionigbu.it/libreria/lunico-conforto-nella-vita-e-nella-morte/

Spanish edition: *El Único Consuelo en la Vida y en la Muerte: la Fe y la Esperanza en la Pandemia*, published by Pensamiento Cristiano. Go to: http://pensamientocristiano.com/

Preface

The spring of 2020 will be remembered in history for the pandemic caused by the COVID-19 virus. Through this pandemic, humanity has been experiencing a period of remarkable disorientation. As this book is being published, we still don't know how or when mankind will be able to return to the normal flow of life's activities in relative security and liberty.

Apart from the shocking video clips of intensive care units from hospitals all over the world, perhaps the most vivid images showing the distress which the whole of humanity is experiencing are those of empty cities. With notable effort Andrea Bocelli, the Italian tenor, tried to bring the cities to life again with his magnificent voice in his Easter performance in front of the Duomo of Milan, where, among other pieces, he sang *Amazing Grace*. This exhibition, however, proved to be just a ripple, enjoyed by millions of people in lockdown, behind their closed windows, in front of their TV, computer and smartphone screens, each on their own; this time without applause.

This desolate backdrop brought to mind to the three authors of this little booklet (an Englishman, an Italian and a Spaniard) the age-old question to ask oneself, and hopefully those friends who will be willing to consider it: *what is the only comfort in life and in death?*

It is an unavoidable question for all of us, whether Christian or not, a question which does not differentiate between the two realities to which it refers: life and death. In the surreal context in which we are now living, life and death are not counterposed, but are in continuity. Economic activities die, the infected body's capacity to react to the virus dies, solidarity with the dying dies and, in the end, as breath itself dies, so too does hope.

What can we believe and hope for in times of a coronavirus epidemic?

We wanted to face this question with the resources to hand and with what we hold dearest as Christians and believers: '*Christ, our hope of glory*'. Consequently, this is a book about hope: how to catch sight of hope in the midst of the pandemic (Pablo Martinez), how to live with hope in this time of crisis (Jonathan Lamb), and how to protect hope against the insinuations of suffering and evil (Giacomo Carlo Di Gaetano). We are three friends from the three European countries most impacted by the pandemic, who share the same convictions and certainties about true hope.

The title of the book comes from the first article of a Confession of Faith at the time of the Reformation, the Heidelberg Catechism (1563). The initial question, getting the catechist started towards the discovery of the Christian faith, succeeded in tying together anguish and hope, death and life. The answer to this question, which we bring to your attention here, sums up the central idea of the meditations which follow.[1]

Question: *What is your only comfort in life and death?*
Answer:[2] *That I am not my own,[3] but belong with body and soul, both in life and in death,[4] to my faithful Saviour Jesus Christ.[5] He has fully paid for all my sins*

---

1   At the end of the book the questions and answers are considered again in the form of a guide to discover and live the Christian hope.

2   The following are the Biblical references relating to the answer:

3   1 Corinthians. 6:19-20.

4   Romans 14:7-9.

5   1 Corinthians 3:23; Titus 2:14.

with His precious blood,[6] and has set me free from all the power of the devil.[7] He also preserves me in such a way[8] that without the will of my heavenly Father not a hair can fall from my head;[9] indeed, all things must work together for my salvation.[10] Therefore, by His Holy Spirit He also assures me of eternal life[11] and makes me heartily willing and ready from now on to live for Him.[12]

Giacomo Carlo Di Gaetano

---

6   1 Peter 1:18-9; 1 John 1:7; 2:2.

7   John 8:34-6; Hebrews 2:14-5; 1 John 3:8.

8   John 6:39, 40; 10:27-30; 2 Thessalonians 3:3; 1 Peter 1:5.

9   Matthew 10:29-31; Luke 21:16-18.

10 Romans 8:28.

11 Romans 8:15, 16; 2 Corinthians 1:21-2; 5:5; Ephesians 1:13-4.

12 Romans 8:14; 1 John 3:3.

1. Finding Hope:
Trust Triumphs over Fear

Dr Pablo Martinez

He who dwells in the shelter of the Most High
will abide in the shadow of the Almighty.
I will say to the LORD, 'My refuge and my fortress,
my God, in whom I trust' (Ps. 91:1-2 ESV).

'I need the sun to shine again in my life. It's as if night had fallen suddenly and now I need light, something to give me hope'. These words were confided to me by a woman whose family has been severely assailed by the coronavirus. Her desperation brought to my mind the words of Miguel de Unamuno,[1] someone who had also experienced suffering at first hand within his own

---

1   A Spanish philosopher considered by many as the most influential of the 20th century.

family: 'Despair is the soil from which the true hope is, and always has been, born.'[2]

We live in days of anxiety and uncertainty. The whole world is in fear. Suddenly we have become aware of the fragility of life. What will happen tomorrow? The strength in which people believed they were safe has turned into weakness, there are cracks in the rock and we feel vulnerable. People look for a message of serenity and tranquillity, but above all a message of hope, because 'hope is to human existence what oxygen is to the lungs'.[3]

A crisis situation such as the one we are experiencing shakes our philosophy of life and weakens our self-sufficiency. This forces us to seek refuge in secure values. In financial areas, people draw on gold when the stock market crashes. What is the equivalent of 'gold' in our life? *Where can we put our trust?* This is the key question.

Christians believe that the secure value *par excellence*, 'the gold' to turn to, is faith – faith in Christ. The apostle Peter wrote, 'your faith [is] of greater worth than gold' (1 Pet. 1:7). And we believe this because the Christian faith responds to the deepest desires of the human

2   Quoted by P. Lain Entralgo, *Esperanza en Tiempos de Crisis* (*Hope in Times of Crisis*), (Galaxia, Gutenberg, 1973), p. 65.

3   Emil Brunner, *Esperanza Eterna* (*Eternal Hope*), (Westminster Press: Philadelphia, 1954).

being and fulfils their greatest needs: *identity* (Who am I?), *purpose* (What am I here for?), *hope* (What happens after death?). For this reason, we endorse the words of Teresa de Ávila, the great Spanish mystic, and say: 'If you have God, what do you lack? If you lack God, what do you have?'

The Bible, God's open letter to humankind, teaches us the path that leads to trust in a time of crisis. Psalm 91 is, in this sense, one of the most encouraging texts in all of Scripture. Sometimes called the *Triumphal Hymn of Trust*, it is a gem. It has breathed encouragement and peace into millions of believers in the midst of trial. According to some commentators, it was written in the midst of an epidemic of pestilence. The circumstances were similar to those we are experiencing today. Its message, therefore, is very relevant to our current pandemic situation.

It can be summed up in one sentence: *trust triumphs over fear*. The text presents the journey from anxiety and fear to confidence, in three expressions, and ends with the guarantee of God Himself in a memorable epilogue:

> 'My God' – what God *is* for me
> 'He will deliver you' – what God *does* for me
> 'I will trust' – my answer

1. 'My God' – the character of God

The psalm begins with a dazzling description of the character of God. Up to four different names are mentioned in the opening two verses to explain who God is and what He is like. What a formidable entrance gate to trust! According to the psalmist, God is the Most High, the Almighty, the LORD (*Yahweh*) and the Sublime God (*Elohim*).

The awareness of God's greatness, the foundation of our confidence

We could paraphrase a popular proverb and say *'tell me what your God is like and I will tell you what your trust is like'*. In the hour of fear, the first step is to lift up your eyes to heaven, to look at God and contemplate His greatness and sovereignty. By so doing, the psalmist experiences that God is *his shelter, his shadow, his hope and his fortress*. The portrait of God in 'four dimensions' heralds a quadruple blessing! Truly knowing God's character is the starting point in the journey towards trust. It is our first need and privilege.

God the great unknown

One of the features of postmodernity is the ignorance of God, in the double sense of the word ignorance – not knowing and not wanting to know. Many people today reject God without knowing anything about Him; in fact, what they reject is their idea of God, a God who is merely the fruit of their imagination. This has been the experience of not a few illustrious atheists. 'I don't think God exists, but if He did exist, He would be my enemy', said someone who had not read a single page of the Bible. He was back from a journey that he hadn't even started.

Know and acknowledge God: 'Sapit qui Deum sapit'

'He is wise who is wise towards God.' This inscription adorns the entrance of the oldest College chapel at Cambridge University, one of the temples of human knowledge. How far removed is this spirit from us today!

The truly wise person not only knows, but recognizes their limitations, they are humble in their wisdom. The philosopher Karl Popper reproached contemporary intellectuals for their 'lack of modesty' and emphasized the need to acknowledge that we do not know everything.[4] The previously mentioned Unamuno, who was a profound connoisseur of the Bible, said: 'The beginning of wisdom is the knowledge of God' (no doubt

---

4   A speech delivered at the Menéndez Pelayo International University, Santander, Spain, in July 1991.

an echo of Proverbs 1:7). Knowing and acknowledging God are inseparable.

A personal God: 'my God'

Notice, however, that the psalmist refers to Him as MY God. That little word, 'my', provides a unique perspective and changes many things: the God of the psalmist is a personal, close God, who intervenes in his life and cares about his fears and needs. *For the Christian, God is not a distant 'He', but a near 'You'.*

Here we have one of the most distinctive features of the Christian faith: God is not only the Almighty, the creator of the Universe, but also the intimate Father, the Abba ('Dad') who loves me and protects me. This is our great privilege: God takes care of us, as a father does with his son, because in Christ we are made children of God: 'Because you are sons, God sent the Spirit of his Son into our hearts, the Spirit who calls out, *"Abba*, Father"' (Gal. 4:6). This unique combination of the transcendence and the immanence of God, His sovereignty and His closeness, is only found in Christianity.

Sensitivity and solidity: 'feathers and shields'

The psalmist describes this experience with a beautiful metaphor: 'He will cover you with his feathers, and under his wings you will find refuge' (Ps. 91:4). As the bird cares for its newborn babies, so God cares for His children.

There is an element of tenderness, warmth, and care. Note, however, that God's protection does not end here. The sensitivity of the breeding goes together with the strength of the shield. It is actually a double shield: 'His truth shall be your shield and buckler' (NKJV).[5]

The term 'truth' here does not refer to a body of revealed doctrines, but rather describes the faithfulness of God. The psalmist comes to say: 'Your fidelity is my shield.' As he stated in the beginning (vv. 1-2), the psalmist's confidence is not in any human resource, but in a divine one.

This double metaphor powerfully describes the unique combination of qualities in the character of the God of the Bible: the tenderness of the loving Father and the solidity of the Almighty, the Lord of the Universe.

2. 'He will deliver you' – God's providence

> For he will deliver you from the snare of the fowler and from the deadly pestilence .... his faithfulness is a shield and buckler. You will not fear ... the pestilence that stalks in darkness, nor the destruction that wastes at noonday ... no evil shall be allowed to befall you, no plague come near your tent (Ps. 91:3-6, 10 ESV).

---

5   The buckler was a shield made of very resistant leather, which covered the thorax, especially protecting the heart.

We come to the heart of the psalm: *God's protection in practice*. The awareness of God's greatness must be followed by the *awareness of God's providence*. What God *is* for me is followed naturally by what God *does* for me.

We are facing a crucial, decisive point in the experience of faith. If we understand it well, it will be a source of peace and serenity, but if we misinterpret it, we can fall into mistakes and extremes, or feel frustrated with God. This is why we need to consider in some detail a unique aspect of this psalm.

The devil's manipulation

It is significant that the devil tempted Jesus (Matt. 4:6, Luke 4:9-10) with a double quote from Psalm 91: 'For he will command his angels concerning you to guard you ... On their hands they will bear you up, lest you strike your foot against a stone' (Ps. 91:11-2 ESV). Satan could have chosen many texts from the Scriptures. Why does he quote this psalm?

A basic principle of biblical interpretation is that a text out of context is a pretext. This is exactly what the devil did: he manipulated the Word, presented a half truth, and thus distorted the promises of divine protection. It is a temptation much in evidence today! We must be wary of super-spirituality and super-faith. It can be a way of tempting God, as Jesus' forceful response to Satan teaches us: 'You shall not tempt the Lord your God' (Matt. 4:7 NKJV).

Trusting the Almighty does not exempt us from acting responsibly and wisely

Faith and prudence are not incompatible; rather they complement and enhance each other. The Bible often associates prudence (the wise man), with spiritual maturity (the God-fearing man). Remember the illustration of the wise and the foolish builders where Jesus identifies the wise man with the one who obeys the Word of God (Matt. 7:24-7).

The devil is particularly interested in our interpreting God's Word in a biased way, especially God's promises. He knows well that this is the most effective way to bring about the shipwreck of faith or the rejection of God.

We now move to consider in detail the mighty protective action of God. The psalmist highlights two aspects: it is a broad protection and it is supernatural.

Broad-spectrum protection

> For He will deliver you from the snare of the fowler and from the deadly pestilence … You will not fear the terror of the night, nor the arrow that flies by day, nor the pestilence that stalks in darkness, nor the destruction that wastes at noonday (Ps. 91:3-6 ESV).

God's protection for the psalmist covers the most varied situations, and occurs in any circumstance. Four examples are mentioned:

- 'The snare of the fowler': this is a metaphor to illustrate the 'traps' or deceits in which one can be inadvertently involved because of others. It alludes to problems in human relationships.
- 'The deadly pestilence' and 'the pestilence that stalks in darkness': the diseases that attack the body, or physical ailments. There was an idea in ancient times that diseases were transmitted at night.
- 'The terror of night': the disease that affects the mind, such as anxiety or panic.
- 'The arrow that flies by day ... or destruction that wastes at noonday': dangers that come from war or any human agent. It might also be equivalent to accidental dangers.

Supernatural protection

> For he will command his angels concerning you to guard you in all your ways. On their hands they will bear you up, lest you strike your foot against a stone. You will tread on the lion and the adder; the young lion and the serpent you will trample underfoot (Ps. 91:11-13 ESV).

In the midst of this catalogue of dangers God does not spare any effort to protect us, so much so that He uses His angels. This protection ranges from the smallest dangers – 'stumbling on a stone' – to the greatest – 'the lion, the asp, the dragon'.

In our rationalist world any reference to angels may seem outdated, simply a myth. But who does not remember situations in which we were delivered from danger in an 'incredible' way? At the last moment, *in extremis*, something happened that made us emerge unscathed from that situation. Are we able to discern the supernatural hand of God in these 'incredible' events? If we keep our eyes open we will discover a miraculous element in God's care for those who love and trust Him. Angels are not a myth, they are a spiritual reality, active today as much as twenty centuries ago (Heb. 1:14).

At this point, a question may arise from a heart full of pain and perplexity: Why was this not my case? Why did God allow so much suffering in my life? A proper answer goes beyond the purpose of this chapter,[6] but some considerations may help us.

---

6   In chapter 3 Giacomo Carlo Di Gaetano deals with this question in more detail. I also develop this theme in my book, *A Thorn in the Flesh* (IVP, 2007).

It is not a comprehensive insurance policy

> God will deliver you ... I will rescue you ... I will deliver you (vv. 3, 14 and 15).

The key word is 'to deliver'. What does the sentence *'God will deliver you'* actually mean? The same expression is used in Joseph's life: God 'delivered him out of all his troubles' (Acts 7:10 NKJV), and yet the patriarch had to go through many valleys of shadow and death. God *did not protect him* from the trial, but He *rescued him* from it.

As Spurgeon said, 'It is not possible for those who are loved by God to be free from all evil'. The great English preacher knew what he was talking about; the cholera epidemic of 1854 in London decimated his church, taking half of his parishioners. *Faith does not guarantee the absence of trial, but it does guarantee victory over trial.* But what kind of victory?

God's presence at our side is our victory

The eyes of faith make us see that the most important thing in this world is not health, not even physical life, but that 'your faith may not fail'. Faith is the greatest treasure to keep. Therefore, our greatest desire is not the absence of tribulation, but the presence of Christ with us in the tribulation (as we will see in a moment).

A text from Isaiah explains this idea with a powerful metaphor:

> When you pass through the waters, **I will be with you**; and through the rivers, they shall not overwhelm you; when you walk through fire you shall not be burned, and the flame shall not consume you (Isa. 43:2 ESV).

God does not promise that we will come out of the waters dry or emerge unharmed by the fire, but He assures us that neither the river will drown us nor the flame will destroy us because 'I will be with you'. The hardest experience is not suffering itself, but loneliness in suffering, and absolute loneliness is to be separated from God. This is why Jesus on the cross exclaimed, 'My God, my God, why have you forsaken me?' (Matt. 27:46).

Someone once said, 'Hell is the place where God does not speak any more'.[7] It is for this reason that we can affirm that the presence of Christ at our side during the hour of trial is our victory. It is the triumph to which the apostle Paul refers when he states 'in all these things (trials) *we are more than conquerors* through him who loved us... for I am convinced that (nothing) will be able to separate us from the love of God that is in Christ Jesus our Lord' (Rom. 8:37-9).

---

7   The phrase is attributed to Dostoevsky.

Thus, faith in Christ is not a vaccine against all evil, but a guarantee of total security, the security that 'if God is for us, who can be against us?' (Rom. 8:31). This psalm is not a promise of complete immunity, but a declaration of full trust. This leads us to consider the third theme.

3. My answer – 'I will trust'

After contemplating the character of God, both what He is to him and His providence – what He does in his life – the psalmist now proclaims firmly: 'My God, in whom I trust.'

It is a logical sequence. The psalmist has come to know who God really is – 'because he knows my name', the Lord declares (v. 14). Such knowledge leads the Psalmist to love – 'he loves me' (v. 14), and, in turn, that love leads him to trust. Trust is a response to love, and love, in turn, is expressed by trust. This reciprocity is a mirror of the Christian experience of faith. Faith in God, like love, means encounter, embrace and trust. It begins with an encounter with Jesus, 'the image of the invisible God', and is nurtured by His love and sustained by trust.

This trust in God's protection is expressed in three ways. In every trial I trust that *God knows, God controls, and God cares (for me).*

Chance is not the force that moves the world. In the life of the children of God nothing happens without His knowledge and consent. We certainly live in an evil world, but not in a world without control or constraint. The last word does not belong to the prince of this world, the devil, but to the King eternal, immortal, invisible (1 Tim. 1:17).

Now 'at present we do not see everything subject to them. But we do see Jesus … now crowned with glory and honour' (Heb. 2:8-9). In this vision of the victorious Christ lies the certainty of our faith and the foundation of our confidence. It is the confidence that lightens our darkness and overcomes all fear in the hour of trial.

A well-known hymn begins: 'Why should I feel discouraged, why should the shadows come? … When Jesus is my portion, my constant friend is he. His eye is on the sparrow, and I know he watches me'.[8]

The hymn's author, Civilla Martin, was inspired by the experience of a disabled woman, bedridden for 20 years, whose husband, also disabled, could only be moved in a wheelchair. One day Civilla asked her if she was ever discouraged. 'How can I be if God, my heavenly Father, watches over each little bird? I know that He loves me and watches over me.' This woman found her strength to live in the text where Jesus affirms:

> Are not two sparrows sold for a penny? Yet not one of them will fall to the ground outside your Father's

---

8   Civilla Martin, 'His Eye is on the Sparrow'.

care. And even the very hairs of your head are all numbered. So don't be afraid; you are worth more than many sparrows (Matt. 10:29-31; see also Luke 12:6-7).

What an encouraging and consoling promise! But we should notice that it is preceded by a key warning: 'Do not be afraid of those who kill the body but cannot kill the soul' (Matt.10:28). In His supreme wisdom Jesus warns us that we must put any trial in its right perspective, remembering the really important priorities of life.

Life on this earth is a precious treasure, but it is not the supreme treasure. The supreme good is eternal life. Health is important, but spiritual health, faith in Christ, is even more important. Suffering always pushes us to review our values and priorities: 'So we fix our eyes not on what is seen, but on what is unseen, since what is seen is temporary, but what is unseen is eternal' (2 Cor. 4:18).

As we have already anticipated, the greatest loss that we can experience on this earth is not physical life, but eternal life. For this reason the Lord Jesus prepares Peter for a time of intense suffering with these words:

Simon, Simon, Satan has asked to sift all of you as wheat. But I have prayed for you, Simon, that your faith may not fail (Luke 22:31-2).

4. The faithfulness of God in action

> 'Because he loves me', says the LORD, 'I will rescue him; I will protect him, for he acknowledges my name. He will call on me, and I will answer him; I will be with him in trouble, I will deliver him and honour him. With long life I will satisfy him and show him my salvation' (Ps. 91:14-6).

By way of conclusion, it is God Himself who speaks at the end of the psalm. To a firm declaration of trust, God responds with an even firmer commitment to fulfil His promises. The last three verses become the climax, the pearl within the jewel, since God's declaration constitutes the guarantee of the psalmist. What an amazing epilogue! If so far we have seen *the providence of God protecting*, now we see *the faithfulness of God fulfilling* His promises.

It is worth noticing the structure of the poem. At the beginning the psalmist speaks in the first person and describes his own experience of faith, what God is to him (vv. 1,2). Then he uses the word 'you' to explain what God is to the reader (vv. 3-13). But this expression of trust would be incomplete without a final guarantee. And for this reason God 'signs' the psalm with a statement as splendid as was the dazzling initial portrait of His character in the opening verses.

God's commitment begins with two sentences introduced by the expression *'because'*: 'Because he has set his love upon me... because he has known my name' (NKJV). This is an important detail. We find here 'the secret' of divine protection. These two expressions – 'because' – are *not conditions*, but *explanations*. They are not clauses; it is simply the logic of events. Experiencing the promises of God is the natural consequence of 'dwelling in the shelter of the Most High'. Outside this shelter, the protective effects are not guaranteed.

God Himself is here ratifying the core of our faith as a relationship of love. He who decides to 'put his love in God' and 'know (recognize) his name' does so voluntarily, not by obligation. It is a love response to the love of God. The psalmist has already stated it earlier: 'Because you have made the LORD, who is my refuge, Even the Most High, your dwelling place' (v. 9 NKJV). Dwelling in the presence of God is a personal decision, a choice. I choose God to be my 'dwelling place'. *To have God as 'my house' is both a spiritual experience and a way of life.*

In the opening verses we saw a fourfold blessing flowing from the character of God; now a whole cascade of blessings arise for those who decide to live in the shelter of the Most High. It is as if God has opened the doors of heaven to pour out all the treasures of His faithfulness. A formidable *crescendo* of promises assures us that God is for and with us:

> I will rescue him; I will protect him, I will answer him; I will be with him in trouble, I will deliver him and honor him. With long life I will satisfy him and show him my salvation (vv. 14-6).

With these solemn yet heart-warming promises the journey from fear to trust ends. The psalmist feels safe because he dwells in the Shadow of the Almighty. We also feel safe because our life is 'hidden with Christ in God' (Col. 3:3); nothing and no one can destroy it.

This is our faith and our hope: *my life is not at the mercy of a virus, but in the hands of the Almighty God.* Those who live in the shelter of the Most High cannot be torn away from this earth a minute before or a minute after the time that God has appointed. God is the one who marks the hours on the clock of our life.

There is no place for triumphalism, but there is certainly triumph. It is the triumph that the resurrection of Christ assured us with His victory over evil and death. It is the same Christ who tells us today:

> And surely I am with you always, to the very end of the age (Matt. 28:20).

2. Living With Hope
The Foundations of Hope in Life and Death

Jonathan Lamb

There is a well-known story of a traveller in the middle ages who arrived at a village and met three labourers working in a quarry. He spoke with them about their daily work. 'What are you doing?', he asked. 'I'm breaking rocks', the first workman replied. The second man responded, 'I'm earning for my family'. But the third labourer stood tall and, with a glint in his eye, responded, 'I'm building a cathedral.'

The way we live now is greatly influenced by what we believe about the future. This is because our hopes and fears for the future substantially shape the present. They impact our attitudes, our motivations and our commitments. Our expectations of the future determine not only our present emotional well-being, but also shape our present decisions and actions.

Hope is not simply about the future. Hope is life itself.

Hope in the pandemic

The coronavirus pandemic has inevitably raised in our minds many uncertainties about the future. We face these as communities and societies, but they also impact us at the personal level. At the time of writing, these relate to questions about the destiny of the virus, and whether the pandemic will come in successive waves; or how it will impact the poorer and less developed nations of the world, the four million refugees in Turkey, and the vulnerable masses in slums and favellas; or how the pandemic will finally be brought under control. And further, we wonder what economic impact this will have in the years to come, with its global implications as well as personal concerns about our employment and economic well-being. Many commentators express their concerns about the longer term mental health of populations which have endured such a crisis, or the impact of sustained isolation for vulnerable people, or the legacy of domestic abuse and fractured family relationships.

Most significantly, during the pandemic we have experienced the reality of death more keenly. Whereas previously death was mostly out of view, recent events in many European communities have brought us closer to death and dying, raising deeper and more ultimate questions for many of us.

Signals of hope

Paradoxically, during the pandemic there have been signs of hope, positive signals of what the future could look like.

There have been many acts of kindness, as neighbours and even strangers have sought to help the vulnerable or elderly. There has been a growing sense of community, and the importance of inter-dependence. I write this in the UK, where one of our problems – unlike much of Europe – is the tendency to be insular and independent. We don't talk to each other in the shops or on London underground trains. But one UK journalist has written that 'there has been a sudden, shocking outbreak of friendliness in London ... Now people are smiling at each other, grateful for small courtesies. A man I've lived opposite for 20 years introduced himself for the first time.' (She added that our secret weapon as a nation could be that we're excellent at queuing.) For those of us in the UK, it has been inspiring to hear Italians singing together from their balconies.

Then there has also been a greater honouring of low-paid workers – the cleaners, the delivery drivers, the shop workers – who serve the community at some risk whilst others self-isolate. There is a desire to do more to help the homeless; there has been some re-ordering of life to create more quiet reflection and thought, even to reflect on our humanity and our mortality. And as we connect more with the natural world in the quiet and less polluted atmosphere, we have a stronger desire to protect the environment. These are all small signals of hope.

The loss of hope

Nevertheless, it seems that the present crisis has simply added fuel to the fire of existing fears and anxieties about human life and destiny. A senior BBC journalist recently wrote a book whose title gave the game away – *Not Quite World's End* – and which he introduced in the following way:

> Sometimes it seems there are so many threats to our life and prosperity that it's hard to choose which of them to concentrate on. Human existence is becoming a little like one of those video games where you are a soldier dodging down endless corridors with some ludicrously large weapon in

your hands, while enemies of every conceivable description jump out at you from all sides.[1]

And it's true, isn't it? Whether it is the uncertainties of global climate change, the turbulence in the Middle East, the threat from rogue states or terrorism, the economic downturn, the fear of global pandemics – each has contributed to a global mood of uncertainty and insecurity. In his book *The Future*, former US Vice President Al Gore has written about the many challenges we are facing, and he declares that 'the future ... now casts a shadow upon the present'[2]. This is a fault-line in our culture, a deep vulnerability and anxiety that many people express. It's been well said that if you are anxious about what is happening, you need to see a psychiatrist; but if you *aren't* anxious, you *definitely* need to see a psychiatrist.

If there is one thing with which the human heart cannot cope it is the lack of hope. Some years ago, a report about the business community in Wall Street Manhattan commented that many young people leave their desks and laptops to visit the Gypsy Tea Kettle in their lunch break where, for $15, they could have a consultation with a psychic. One 30 year-old business

---

1   John Simpson, *Not Quite World's End* (London: Pan Books, 2008).

2   Al Gore, *The Future* (W.H.Allen, 2013), p. xxiii.

woman was asked why so many did this. She replied: 'Psychics are more valuable than friends. They can see where you're going and give you hope for the future.'

Even before the onset of the 2020 pandemic, many young people across our continent had succumbed to one of today's most prevalent diseases – Europessimism. Social commentators tell us that this generation of young people is more anxious, more uncertain about the future, than recent generations. This is the first generation of young people in a century to have less high hopes than their parents.

And without true hope, people turn to substitutes of all kinds. In a two-page spread about dogs in *The Times* newspaper, several writers spoke about how their canine companions are helping them get through the self-isolation during the pandemic. 'The world feels a better, infinitely more hopeful place when he is by my side', wrote Emily Dean, author of *Everybody Died, So I Got a Dog*. But for others, the substitutes for hope might be the escapist routes of drug and alcohol abuse; it might be self-indulgence, which attempts to maximise on present experience as a way of avoiding thinking about ultimate issues. It might be astrology, or occult practice, or superstition of all kinds, as people become desperate to gain some sense of control over their lives.

The future and the present

The Biblical books which speak most about the future were written to encourage hard-pressed Christians here and now. The apostle Peter is a good example. He knew that hope was right at the heart of the Christian faith. So one of his central aims was to encourage his readers, who were facing pressures and trials of all kinds, by giving them grounds for solid hope in the ultimate future. This would feed back in such a way as to give them confidence – even joy – in the midst of the turmoil and uncertainty they were facing.

Hope is not a sedative, but an injection of adrenaline, a spur for action. And Peter shows that it spans past, present and future. Here is how he begins his first letter:

> Peter, an apostle of Jesus Christ, to God's elect, exiles scattered throughout the provinces of Pontus, Galatia, Cappadocia, Asia and Bithynia, who have been chosen according to the foreknowledge of God the Father, through the sanctifying work of the Spirit, to be obedient to Jesus Christ and sprinkled with his blood: Grace and peace be yours in abundance.
>
> Praise be to the God and Father of our Lord Jesus Christ! In his great mercy he has given us new birth into a living hope through the resurrection of Jesus Christ from the dead, and into an inheritance that can never perish, spoil or fade. This inheritance is kept in heaven for you, who through faith are

shielded by God's power until the coming of the salvation that is to be revealed in the last time (1 Pet. 1:1-5).

1. Hope is embedded in a bigger story

When Peter was writing to the Christians of his day, he was writing to aliens and refugees. You'll notice how he describes them in v1: 'To God's elect, strangers in the world, scattered throughout Pontus, Galatia, Cappadocia, Asia and Bithynia...'

Maybe they were people who had been thrown out of Rome because they didn't belong, and were now scattered across Asia Minor (present-day Turkey), where they didn't belong either. They were a marginalised social class. And Peter uses the idea to say that, in reality, every true Christian believer is a stranger in the world. He describes our calling as sojourners or migrants. We are exiles on a journey, following in the steps of Jesus Himself. So Peter's letter is a traveller's guide for Christian pilgrims who are pressing ahead on a hazardous journey.

His introduction is very significant. 'To God's elect', he underlines as he begins; 'who have been chosen according to the foreknowledge of God the Father, through the sanctifying work of the Spirit, for obedience to Jesus Christ and sprinkling by his blood' (v. 2). He deliberately begins with the core certainty that we belong to God Himself.

The late Stephen Hawking, the mathematician and cosmologist, often received letters and emails from around the world, and one of the most common enquries in his mail bag was the question: *'Can you prove that God does not exist?'* His reply is often quoted: 'We are such insignificant creatures on a minor planet of a very average star in the outer suburbs of one of a hundred thousand million galaxies. So it is difficult to believe in a God that would care about us, or even notice our existence.'[3]

But Peter's opening verses are quite different from Stephen Hawking's cynicism. Peter underlines that you and I are known to God from the very beginning of eternity. We are chosen and loved by Him. And this is truly important for us to grasp, since it is part of the foundation of Christian identity and Christian assurance. This is the bigger story which is the foundation for true hope.

In his book *The Real American Dream: A Meditation on Hope*, Andrew Delbanco underlines that hope manifests itself when our lives become integrated into a larger story. Whilst describing the American dream,

---

3   BBC Radio 4 broadcast celebrating Stephen Hawking's 70th birthday.

his thesis holds good for almost all human cultures – it is the hope of satisfying 'the unquenchable human need to feel connected to something larger than the insular self'. Closer to home, Ivan Krastev has written about threatened populations in Europe which think similarly: 'The nation, not unlike God, is one of humanity's shields against the idea of mortality. It is in the memory of our family and nation that we have hope to continue living after our death.'[4]

Delbanco goes on to explain the central story that has united the American people and become the driving force of hope: in the eighteenth century it was God, in the nineteenth century it was the nation, and in the twentieth century it was the self – hence his concern that he now sees a culture without a coherent story.

> When that story leads somewhere and thereby helps us navigate through life to its inevitable terminus in death, it gives hope ... We must imagine some end to life that transcends our own tiny allotment of days and hours if we are to keep at bay the 'dim, back-of-the-mind suspicion that one may be adrift in an absurd world'.[5]

---

4   Ivan Krastev, *After Europe* (University of Pennsylvania Press, 2020) pp. 50-1.

5   Andrew Delbanco, *The Real American Dream: A Meditation on Hope* (Harvard University Press, 1999), pp. 1-2.

We can see how radical and significant is Peter's assertion that every person who has come to know God through Jesus Christ is part of God's big story which, as we shall see, is a story which extends beyond 'the inevitable terminus of death'.

And Peter's profound good news gives the lie to the oft-quoted statement by the scientist Richard Dawkins, who suggests that we live in a universe 'with no rhyme or reason, no design or purpose – nothing but blind pitiless indifference'.[6] The Christian worldview is not defined merely by the self, by individual stories, nor by a chaotic or random series of historical events, but by an over-arching story which is moving forward to a transformative goal. As Pablo Martinez has written in the previous chapter, chance is not the force which moves the world. In a passage describing the future, when Paul compares his present fragile and temporary body – a 'tent' – with his 'eternal house in heaven', he is very deliberate in stating that this is not random, but planned, something which God had in mind all along. 'Now the one who has fashioned us *for this very purpose* is God', he says, as he describes the future beyond death (2 Cor. 5:5).

---

6   Richard Dawkins, *River Out of Eden* (Phoenix, 1995), p. 133.

Wrapped into God's purpose

Peter explains this in more detail in verse 2, as he describes what it means to be part of God's story. Although the answer appears in theological language which might seem rather impenetrable, at its heart is wonderfully good news about our Christian certainty.

Through the Lord Jesus, our lives have been lifted out of the chaos of the broken story of our world, out of the unfettered invidividualism of our culture, and out of the despair of merely drifting in an absurd world. Now we truly belong, we truly have purpose and direction. We are chosen by the Father, sanctified by the Spirit and cleansed by the blood of Christ (v. 2). All three members of the Trinity are at work, guaranteeing our membership of God's family and wrapping us into God's good purposes.

We know that future hope transforms this present moment, and this is the main theme of this chapter. But we will see from Giacomo Carlo Di Gaetano's chapter that hope is also founded on our present awareness of God's sovereign control of our world and our lives. For Christians, this represents the real story – a story which begins in a past eternity, which includes but transcends our own life span, and which carries us forward to an eternity to come. It is the story of God's loving plan and purpose for men and women, a story of a good but broken creation, a story of God's plan of restoration, a story which helps us 'navigate through life to its inevitable terminus', stretching beyond death to a new heaven and earth.

2. Hope is certain because of a past event

Peter then explains that hope for the future is based on a significant past event. 'In his great mercy he has given us new birth into a living hope through the resurrection of Jesus Christ from the dead' (v. 3).

In English the word hope has come to imply a measure of uncertainty in our everyday conversation. Our hopes are to do with something that has not yet occurred, and so we look at the possibilities and say, 'I hope it will be like this'. 'If I do a modest amount of work I hope I will pass my examinations ... but I'm not entirely sure.' We use the word realising that there are no guarantees. But Christian hope is radically different. It will be realised. It is totally certain. Why? Because it is based on an event which has already happened – *hope through the resurrection of Jesus Christ from the dead'.*

Throughout the New Testament we discover that Jesus' resurrection is pivotal. Slowly the early Christians came to see that the great day of renewal of all things in this universe had begun. The new day had now dawned. And further, they realized that the ultimate future was now certain because of that moment of resurrection.

The Czech novelist, Ivan Klima, wrote about hope in his book *The Spirit of Prague*. 'Because death appears to be the only absolute in human life, all hope is relative, an illusion that helps man make it to the gallows. True hope can only be offered to man by someone able to invest that final necessity with hope, by someone capable of guiding man through the valley of the shadow of death.'[7] And this is the reality which Peter describes. Someone has walked through that valley. Someone has defeated the enemy of death. The Oxford professor C. S. Lewis once described it in dramatic language:

> Jesus has forced open a door that has been locked since the death of the first man. He has met, fought and beaten the king of death. Everything is different because he has done so. This is the beginning of the new creation. A new chapter in cosmic history has opened.[8]

Peter knew this not only as a theological truth, but as something that had transformed his own life. When Jesus died on the cross Peter's hopes died too. But when

---

7   Ivan Klima, *The Spirit of Prague* (London: Granta Books, 1994), p. 81.

8   C. S. Lewis, *Miracles* (Collins Fontana Books, 1970), p. 149.

he met the risen Lord his life was turned round. He realised that in Jesus' victory, God makes all things new – beginning with everyone who puts their faith in Jesus, everyone who is united to Him.

Meeting the risen Christ

The same was true for Jesus' disciples. Luke tells us that, after the crucifixion, Jesus drew alongside the dejected disciples on the road to Emmaus after the events of Jesus' crucifixion, though they failed to recognize who He was. '*We had hoped ...*', the disciples said to Him, a poignant phrase with which we might identify, expressing their sadness and disillusionment as they travelled away from Jerusalem, away from hope. 'We had hoped that he was the one who was going to redeem Israel' (Luke 24:21). And through opening the scriptures, Jesus revealed Himself to them – He was risen, He was the promised deliverer, He truly was the redeemer. Other disciples were in lockdown: 'the doors were locked for fear of the Jews'. And Jesus appeared to them in the room – He stood among them and said, 'Peace be with you' (John 20:19). In our own periods of sadness or despair, or in times of lockdown, self-isolation, or loneliness, the living Lord can speak His word of shalom into troubled hearts.

Why does this matter?

One of the features of the global pandemic has been the greater awareness of the fragility of life, and the inevitablity of death. And we know that many people, whatever their culture, are deeply afraid of death. Of course, there has been an obsession with the idea of immortality for centuries, but today it's a serious research industry.

Stephen Cave has written about the quest for immortality, but explains that 'despite the best efforts of science and technology and the very real improvements in life expectancy that have been achieved, the terrifying prospect of death still hangs over us.' [9] His language is significant: 'the terrifying prospect'. Some psychologists have worked on 'terror management theory', suggesting that most of what we do and most of what we believe is motivated by the fear of death. An everyday example is given by the sociologist Zygmunt Bauman, who says that the medicalisation of daily life – our emphasis on diets, exercise, vitamin supplements – is now the primary strategy for suppressing the fear of death.

Indeed, there are now websites which will help you calculate the date of your death. You type in details of age, health, family background and so on, and there you have the prediction. But they are not too popular.

9   Stephen Cave, *Death: Why We Should be Grateful for It* (New Scientist Issue 2887, October 2012), pp. 38-40.

Most people don't want to know; they don't want to be reminded of that terrifying prospect.

We have said that our lives now are shaped substantially by what we believe the future holds, and this is specially true with regard to the prospect of death. It is said that a philosophy that can't make sense of death, can't make sense of life either. And it is here that God's big story – and specifically Peter's reference to Jesus' resurrection – becomes so profound and significant.

Death overcome

Peter not only wrote this, but he also preached this. In one of the earliest Christian sermons, Peter declared that Jesus' death was no accident but part of God's big story, and he used a penetrating phrase with regard to the final enemy of death.

> This man was handed over to you by God's deliberate plan and foreknowledge; and you, with the help of wicked men, put him to death by nailing him to the cross. But God raised him from the dead, freeing him from the agony of death, because it was impossible for death to keep its hold on him (Acts 2:23-4).

Peter has spoken in these verses of God's plan that Jesus should be put to death. This was God's purpose from the very beginning, because Jesus' death was the means by which the penalty for our sins was paid, and therefore the means by which God forgives our sins. I wonder if you know this to be true in your own life? This is the good news of the Christian gospel: it is not what we do, but what is done by Jesus Himself. In summarising the Christian message, Paul tells us what really matters: 'Christ died *for our sins* ... he was buried ... he was raised on the third day' (1 Cor. 15:4). And so for each of us who turns to Him in repentance and faith, Jesus' death has secured our forgiveness. Our sin is taken away and we are freely forgiven.

And how do we know this to be true?

Paul explains further: 'If Christ has not been raised, our preaching is useless and so is your faith ... If Christ has not been raised, your faith is futile; you are still in your sins' (1 Cor. 15:14, 17). In other words, if Jesus was still in the tomb, then the apostles are false witnesses, and we are unforgiven. But if Christ was raised to new life, as both Peter and Paul declare, then this assures us that Jesus' death has achieved God's purpose – everyone who puts their faith in Jesus is truly forgiven!

And further, death is now a broken power. Back in his letter, Peter explains that Christ's resurrection spells hope not simply because *He* lives, but because He has also introduced *us* into that new life. 'He has given us new birth into a living hope through the resurrection of Jesus Christ from the dead' (v. 3). Our new life, a life which extends into eternity, is now totally guaranteed and secure because of Jesus' resurrection.

Few of us will easily forget the news footage of mass graves of Covid-19 victims joining other 'unclaimed dead' on Hart Island, off the Bronx in New York, or coffins stacked in a Madrid ice rink, or the make-shift morgues being erected in car parks. It chills the spine of so many in the western world, who try to keep the terrifying prospect of death at bay.

The Christian message speaks directly to this. To be a Christian is not to belong to some strange sub-culture, a club we have joined because we all think the same thing. We are truly given new life by God. In Jesus' victory, God makes all things new, beginning with everyone who puts their faith in Jesus, who died and rose again. And this new life is now totally guaranteed and secure because of Jesus' resurrection. The ultimate future is now certain because of that moment of resurrection. Nothing in your life or mine could be more sure.

3. Hope anticipates a secure future

> He has given us new birth into a living hope … and into an inheritance that can never perish, spoil or fade. This inheritance is kept in heaven for you (1 Pet. 1:4).

My wife and I are now at the stage in life when our three daughters, with good humour, have already suggested an allocation of our modest possessions between them. One of them suggested that the books go to our youngest daughter, the house goes to the oldest, and the third gets the elderly parents to look after! The New Testament uses the word 'inheritance' to express the legal claim which the heir already has on the property, even while the father is still alive.

So Peter is encouraging Christians in an uncertain world to remember that their future is secure. Our name is already on our full inheritance. It is waiting for us, 'ready to be revealed' (v. 5). The resurrection of Jesus, and our new birth in Him, means that God's salvation is completed, perfect, kept for us by God Himself. This is quite unlike the unfounded utopian dreams of some ideologies. God's purpose for our future is already a reality. It is a secure possession.

Some suggest Peter is making an allusion to the Old Testament story of God's people called out of Egypt. There is a *promised land* prepared for us too, Peter implies. And it is kept safely by God. It can't perish, spoil or fade. Verse 9 describes 'the *goal* of our faith' (again, notice the language of plan and purpose), 'the salvation of our souls.'

The beginning of the real story

That is the great day to which we are heading. Paul writes about this big story, with its eventual goal, in a remarkable statement about God's mission. He describes God's ultimate purpose: 'to bring unity to all things in heaven and on earth under Christ' (Eph. 1:10).

Despite its apparent simplicity, here is a remarkable all-embracing vision, a perspective which shapes our understanding of the world and its future. Paul uses a mathematical term when he signals that all things will be 'summed up' to find their unity and completion in Jesus Christ. When we 'add up', most of us place the total at the bottom. Our Excel sheets do so automatically. But the Greeks literally did '*add up*' – and they placed the total at the top. God's purpose is that everything will find its unity and completion in Jesus Christ; everything will be summed up and brought to perfection in Him. That is the eventual goal of God's purpose of salvation.

Space does not allow us to elaborate on what this vision represents, but we should note the forward trajectory of the story. The resurrection of Jesus points towards the restoration of all things which Paul is describing. 'The resurrection is not, as it were, a highly peculiar event within this *present* world (though it is that as well); it is, principally, the defining event of the *new* creation, the world which is being born with Jesus.'[10]

We are reminded every day that death is still with us, but the final pages of the Bible point us to what that future will hold.

> And I heard a loud voice from the throne saying, 'Look! God's dwelling-place is now among the people, and he will dwell with them and be their God. He will wipe every tear from their eyes. There will be no more death or mourning or crying or pain, for the old order of things has passed away' (Rev. 21:3-4).

This, as C. S. Lewis captured in his *Chronicles of Narnia*, is 'the beginning of the real story'. This present life, he said, is the cover and title page of the Great Story, 'which goes on for ever: in which every chapter is better than the one before.'[11]

The global pandemic should be something which provokes us to weep. We often feel the brokenness of our world, and should identify with its pain and sorrow. In his book about the death of his son, Nicholas Wolterstorff said: 'I shall look at the world through tears. Perhaps I

---

10   Tom Wright, *Surprised by Hope* (SPCK, 2007), p. 84.
11   C. S. Lewis, *The Last Battle* (HarperCollins, 1956), p. 221.

shall see things that dry-eyed I could not see'.[12] This is important for all of us.

But Peter's second letter also encourages us to lift our eyes and look for a new heaven and a new earth – *'the home of righteousness'* (2 Pet. 3:13). It will not spoil, it cannot be defiled, and there will be no shred of bitterness, no hate, no arrogance, no greed. There will be no more pain, or death, or tears. There will be nothing to spoil our eventual home.

4. Hope transforms our present experience

Critics of the Christian faith often suggest that the focus on a future home lessens a resolve to address the challenges of the present. Like the 'preppers' – the growing number of people who have readied themselves for Doomsday – Christians, they say, are effectively withdrawing into their bunkers as they wait for the End Times. But history and personal experience demonstrate that this is most certainly not the case.

> The Christian hope of heaven raises our horizons and elevates our expectations – inviting us to behave on earth in the light of this greater reality. The true believer is not someone who disengages

---

12   Nicholas Wolterstorff, *Lament for a Son* (SPCK, 1997), p. 26.

with this world in order to focus on heaven but someone who tries to make this world like heaven.[13]

This is precisely why those with living hope must engage fully with a practical commitment to care for the vulnerable in the global pandemic, play their part in communities and societies, love their neighbour and pray for the resolution to the crisis. We began by describing the three labourers on the building site, whose end goal transformed their present work. And the apostle Paul made this point clearly when he wrote his great chapter about the future hope of resurrection. After an incredible apologetic which undergirds our certainty about that future, here is his deliberate exhortation about the present:

> Therefore, my dear brothers and sisters, stand firm. Let nothing move you. Always give yourselves fully to the work of the Lord, because you know that your labour in the Lord is not in vain (1 Cor. 15:58).

This has been seen throughout the past two millennia. 'The Christians who did most for the present world were just those who thought most of the next.'[14]

If you read the rest of this short letter you'll discover that Peter is a realist. He isn't attempting to escape the

---

13   Alister McGrath, *Mere Discipleship* (SPCK, 2018), p. 141.
14   C. S. Lewis, *Mere Christianity* (HarperCollins, 2002), p. 134.

sordid present by promising a glorious future. He knows all about the present struggles of Christian disciples. So he reminds us that Christian hope, based on the resurrection of Jesus, helps us face this present reality. The paragraph we are exploring explains several ways in which that happens.

First, Peter describes God's powerful protection

> Who through faith are shielded by God's power until the coming of the salvation that is ready to be revealed in the last time (1 Pet. 1:5).

This encouragement is essential, because all Christians are under pressure. Young believers might wonder if they will be able to keep it up; older Christians might fear that they might not finally make it to their home in heaven. So Peter says, we are kept by God's power. The word Peter uses has a military ring: we are *'shielded'*, we are *'kept under guard'*, so that no matter what is thrown at us, no matter what enemies are ranged against us, no matter how battered we feel in experiencing pressures and griefs of all kinds, God promises to protect us.

This doesn't mean that suffering disappears, that we automatically beam up from the present mess into our secure mother ship. Christians are not immune from the sorrows of this fallen world. Jesus never promised to take us out of troubled circumstances, just as we have seen from the realism of Psalm 91 which Pablo Martinez has explained earlier. For sure, we are secure as we trust God, but we do not escape the difficulties which are common to humanity. God's purpose is not to bypass difficulties, but to transform them.

Second, Peter describes patient endurance

> These [trials] have come so that the proven genuineness of your faith – of greater worth than gold, which perishes even though refined by fire – may result in praise, glory and honor when Jesus Christ is revealed (1 Pet. 1:7).

Sometimes the greatest challenge we face is coping with the long haul. The global pandemic has resulted in the lockdown of homes and businesses, with all of the uncertainties and frustrations this brings. We don't know how long we must endure the global pandemic. We experience the same in other spheres of life, whether living with difficult relationships, or long-term illness, or sustained pressure at work.

Peter describes a paradox which, as we look back over months or years, we understand to be true: these trials can have the positive effect of producing patient endurance, maturing our faith like gold refined by fire. Peter says this will have long-term benefits too:

it will result in praise to God and glory for the faithful believer on that final day (v. 7). It's another aspect of the transforming power of hope.

Third, Peter describes joyful anticipation

> [You] are shielded by God's power until the coming of the salvation that is ready to be revealed in the last time ... in all this you greatly rejoice ... [you] are filled with inexpressible and glorious joy (1 Pet. 1:5-6, 8).

Peter is describing the steady joyfulness of those who know what the future holds; those who, despite suffering grief of all kinds, know that evil has lost the initiative. It no longer rules over us, since we are shielded, and it will one day be done away with when our final salvation will be revealed. This explains the paradox of rejoicing in the midst of suffering, something which both Paul and James also wrote about.[15]

Peter refers to this profound depth of joy later in his letter: 'Rejoice that you participate in the sufferings of Christ, so that you may be overjoyed when his glory is revealed' (1 Pet. 4:13). After all, one day we will see Jesus. Of course, we haven't seen Him as Peter did, but we can be filled with inexpressible joy through our living

---

15   Romans 5:3-5; 12:12; 2 Corinthians 6:10; Colossians 1:24; James 1:2-4.

relationship with Him here and now. We can anticipate that heavenly joy, even in the midst of evil. We know that this world is not destined for the dustbowls of infinity, but that God's purpose – already underway through the resurrection of Christ – is a new heaven and earth.

So there should be a sense of joyful anticipation as we think about that future, a kind of home-sickness for heaven. I like Jim Packer's illustration, when he says that facing death and nurturing our readiness means that each day should find us like children looking forward to their holidays. When I was young my family had an annual week of holiday in August, on the south coast of England. I was so excited by that prospect, I had my small back pack ready to go many months before! I wonder if you have ever thought of death as an exciting prospect? It's not morose if we truly understand that this life is a preparation for eternity. We need not dodge the issue of death or postpone our heavenly rejoicing. We should anticipate it.

The well known Irish flute player, James Galway, was involved in a car accident some years ago in which he very nearly lost his life. It was a profound experience that forced him to face up to the way in which he was living his life. This is what he wrote:

> I decided that from now on I would play every concert, cut every record, give every TV programme, as though it were my last. I have come to understand that it is never possible to guess what may happen next, and that the important thing is to make sure that every time I play the flute, my performance will be as near perfection and full of true music as God intended, and that I shall not be remembered for a shoddy performance.

We don't know what our immediate future will look like, personally, nationally or globally. There are many uncertainities in our continent, and in our hearts. But we have seen that in a few sentences Peter has introduced us to a living hope that can transform our present life. He urges us to take this hope seriously. It's the most important thing in our lives, so he encourages us to 'set your hope fully on the grace to be given you when Jesus Christ is revealed' (1 Pet. 1:13).

We need not sink into the despair of our society nor be overwhelmed by fear. Rather, we can live our lives joyfully and productively, since we know we are part of God's big story, we are certain of Christ's resurrection, and we eagerly anticipate our future home.

3. Safeguarding Hope
Confronting Suffering and Evil

Giacomo Carlo Di Gaetano

Hope is inextricably tied to the heart of man. In pandemic-stricken Italy, while the virus spread throughout our cities, hospitals and our homes, and as we listened, stunned, to the *Presidente Del Consiglio* (our Prime Minister) announce the lockdown (8 March 2020), the hashtag *#andratuttobene* (everything will be alright) became the catalyst of hope for an entire nation.

We filled our balconies and sang, we applauded doctors and nurses, all the while knowing that this was a collective ritual, the purpose of which was merely emotional. *Speaking frankly, we don't know if everything will be alright;* we aren't sure. Our 'phase 2', much desired by the authorities, is revealing itself every day to be full of uncertainty. Already, on 6 April, a Ministry of Justice official from Piacenza – one of the cities most affected by the pandemic – wrote an article which appeared in the newspaper *Corriere della sera* entitled '*Macerie dentro e fuori, in attesa di una speranza timida e tremante*' – 'Ruins inside and out, waiting for a timid and trembling hope'. He predicted:

> Even when we have passed this terrible phase, we won't be able to live with lightheartedness and the conviction that this evil will no longer return to contaminate our bodies and our minds.

We are unable to ignore that simple and unavoidable saying which reveals the fragility of human hope: *chi di speranza vive, disperato muore* – he who lives only by hope will die in despair.

One way to give our hope greater substance is to base it on solid foundations or surround it with good reasons. During the coronavirus crisis, this specific role has been played by 'science'. Governments receive advice from Scientific Advisory Groups and we all rely on the progress being made by researchers working hard for the discovery of a possible vaccine. Science prescribes our behaviour, manages our expectations and determines the presence, or absence, of hope.

In the Bible hope is also connected to reason. The writer to the Hebrews tells us: 'Now faith is confidence in what we hope for and assurance about what we do not see' (Heb. 11:1), which ties together faith and hope. Biblical hope is directly related to what one's beliefs actually are. It has to do with reasons for 'faith' but, as Jonathan Lamb explained in his chapter, it is a faith tied to facts and events.

The faith of the believer is, in fact, determined by actual events (1 Cor. 15); it is cultivated by the way in which events have been passed on (2 Pet. 1:21) and for this reason it is full of hope (Ps. 78:7). All of this is possible because of the principal protagonist of the Bible, the God of Israel and Father of the Lord Jesus Christ. His mysterious name, revealed to Moses as 'I am who I am' (Exod. 3:14) gives hope 'from generation to generation'. The synthesis of biblical revelation is that without God in the world, the world is *without hope* (Eph. 2:12)!

The pandemic we are facing is a manifestation of what philosophers have called 'natural evil'. John Lennox, who has written about this kind of evil, affirms that for 'earthquakes, tsunamis, tumours and the coronavirus, men are not (directly) responsible'.[1] It is this natural evil, when combined with another type of evil (defined as

---

1   John Lennox, *Where is God in a Coronavirus World?* (The Good Book Company, 2020), p. 14.

'moral', for which humankind *is* responsible), which has always posed a challenge for Christian thought and for Christian hope.

For many women and men these evils are great obstacles to faith: many oppose Christ's message precisely because of the presence of evil in the world. For this reason, the explanations we hear during the pandemic are predominantly reductionist and tend to reduce everything to mere biology. Giorgio Agamben[2], for example, holds that it is only the survival instinct – 'naked life' – which led Italians to accept the lockdown. Meanwhile, another philosopher, Paolo Galimberti, without mincing his words, affirms that at the end of the day it will be biology that will triumph, in as much as 'bios means life'.[3]

---

2   The thesis of Agamben is in his blog on *Quodlibet Publishing House pages* (https://www.quodlibet.it/una-voce-giorgio-agamben).

3   'Christianity spread an optimism in the West which has taught us to think in these terms: the past is bad, the present is redemption, and the future is salvation... It is not so. The future is not the time of salvation, it is not awaited, it is not hopeful. The future is a time just like all the others. There won't be providence which will come to meet us and to resolve all the problems of our passivity. We hope, we wish, we pray: these are all verbs of inaction and passivity', *Riflessioni ai tempi del coronavirus sul senso del futuro*, https://alzogliocchiversoilcielo. blogspot.com/2020/04/umberto-galimberti-riflessioni-ai-tempi.html).

It was the Greek philosopher Epicurus who first threw down the gauntlet, with a challenge that, over the course of the centuries, made the presence of evil in the world the 'rock of atheism'.[4] The strategy of this challenge is clear: if we are not able to provide an 'explanation' for the pandemic, well, we have rendered 'Christian' hope in vain, and we can push it away into the camp of fairy tales that we make up merely to comfort people – *#everythingwillbealright*.

Consequently the entire edifice of the Christian faith becomes an illusion, and we might therefore be distrustful of it, just as Marx, Nietzsche, Freud, and the new atheism teach us. The philosopher Alvin Plantinga maintains that the problem of evil constitutes a true *atheology*, an attempt to demonstrate that theistic convictions are false.[5]

In this chapter I will not try to respond to this atheistic challenge, which hinges on evil and suffering in the

---

4   'God, he says, either wishes to take away evils, and is unable; or He is able, and is unwilling; or He is neither willing nor able, or He is both willing and able. If He is willing and is unable, He is feeble, which is not in accordance with the character of God; if He is able and unwilling, He is envious, which is equally at variance with God; if He is neither willing nor able, He is both envious and feeble, and therefore not God; if He is both willing and able, which alone is suitable to God, from what source then are evils?' (Epicurus, cit. Lactantius, *De ira Dei*).

5   Alvin Plantinga, *God and Other Minds* (Cornell University Press, Ithaca and London, ed. 1990) p. 115.

world. Instead, continuing with the same approach in which Pablo Martinez and Jonathan Lamb describe the reality and effects of Christian hope, I will seek to show how this hope is safe when it is kept secure in an enclosure of the truth which the Bible clearly teaches. For those who reject the message of Christ because of the apparent success of the atheist's arguments, I hope that these truths might provide an incentive to truly consider the Christian gospel.

What are these truths in which we must believe that are related to the presence of evil in the world? We can deduce them directly from Epicurus's challenge:

- The presence of evil in the world, its reality and wickedness;
- The omnipotence (the sovereignty) of God;
- The goodness of God.

To these truths is traditionally added the theme of man's responsibility, or the creature's freedom, to explain how evil entered the world. This theme, however, becomes an attempt to reconcile the three truths listed above. And the reconciliation of these truths has always been the main strategy deployed to respond to the challenge of the atheist or sceptic. However, I find it more useful – both for Christian life and for Christian testimony to those who don't believe – to maintain that these three truths must be believed and confessed rather than reconciled.[6]

Giving up on their reconciliation isn't a weakness. First, it may be useful to point out the warning of many Christian scholars: the attempts to reconcile these three truths often leads to an exaggeration of one of the truths to the detriment of the other two (reductionism). We are given an authoritative testimony of this by a Bible scholar directly confronted with the problem of suffering:

> What we must *not* do is to draw inferences from part of the evidence that contradicts other parts of the evidence. The presence of evil does not function in the Bible so as to deny the goodness of God. The absoluteness of God's sovereign sway never operates so that his ultimacy behind good and evil is entirely symmetrical. Nor does the presence of evil function in such a way as to deny God's sovereignty, or his personal attachment to his covenant people.[7]

Second, the inadequacy of these strategies in reconciling the three truths, constructed throughout the course of

---

6   In this approach I follow in the footsteps of Henri Blocher, *Evil and the Cross: Christian Thought and the Problem of Evil* (IVP Apollos, 1994).

7   D. A. Carson, *How Long, O Lord? Reflections on Suffering and Evil*, (IVP, 1990). The author takes care to highlight the biblical compatibilism between God's sovereignty and human responsibility.

history, and the consequent danger of reductionism, can be seen when they are presented with three simple questions. In the majority of cases these strategies do not give a positive response, and fail to answer fundamental questions:

- Do they take seriously the feelings of the victims?
- Do they obscure or relativize God's sovereignty?
- Do they imply that evil or evils derive from God Himself?

There is a third reason, which we will talk about later, why we should distrust the strategies that, at any cost, try to reconcile the three truths we have mentioned.

For the moment I would like to respond to the question posed at the beginning: *what should we believe and hope in times like these?* When believed and confessed, the teaching of the Bible – even in its complexity – provides reasons that protect Christian hope. But they are also reasons that can be offered to those who find themselves having lost hope: 'the sum of Biblical truths is a trampoline of hope '.

A brief overview of the three biblical truths

The wicked and negative reality of evil

The insidious presence of an invisible virus generates worry and despair: it has revealed itself to be a ruthless virus if you consider the effect it has had on the elderly within our populations. Witnessing this compels us to agree with what the French theologian Henri Blocher affirms: 'Evil is disruption, discontinuity, disorder, alienness; that which defies description in creational terms (except negatively!)'.[8]

The Bible doesn't hesitate to present us with evil in dark colours, thus agreeing completely with the philosopher's most rudimentary analysis of events. No horror is held back, whether natural evil, famine and illnesses of various types, or atrocities and tragic events which shake the lives of the faithful, such as we see in the stories of Naomi and Job. We are shown the distress of man's heart and of all creation 'groaning as in the pains of childbirth' (Rom. 8:18-24).

From the Pauline image of the 'thorn in the flesh' (2 Cor. 12:7), to the clarity of the revelation that the apostle receives, scripture conveys the idea of unalterable

---

8   Henri Blocher, *Evil and the Cross*, p. 103.

suffering.[9] Something isn't right in our world. The awareness of the difference between what *should be* and *what
is* represents the essence of our contemporary dilemma.

The way in which God relates to the presence of evil
in all its forms is similarly instructive. It invites us not
to waver, but to reflect solemnly on the victims of evil,
those whose souls are struck by tragedy, by injustice, and
by violence (such as we see in the discussion between
God and Hagar in Genesis 16). Certainly the Bible helps
us see a future in which 'He will wipe every tear from
their eyes. There will be no more death or mourning
or crying or pain, for the old order of things has passed
away' (Rev. 21:4); but it doesn't hide the suffering voices
that rise throughout the course of history (Pss. 31, 88,
130, etc.), nor the question so full of pathos: 'How long,
LORD, how long?' (Ps. 6:3).

The denunciation of evil in the world is clear in
scripture: *hate what is evil*, Paul affirms (Rom. 12:9),
giving an echo of Isaiah's warning not to mistake evil
for something other than what it is (Isa. 5:20). In His
teaching, Jesus invited us to look at God's initial project,
suggesting: 'it was not this way from the beginning'
(Matt. 19:8). Everyone, believer or not, knows that
scripture presents the events which happened in ages

---

9   Pablo Martinez, *A Thorn in the Flesh*, (IVP, 2007).

past when, we are told, death 'entered into the world'. But that doesn't mean the Bible refuses to talk about the marvellous opposite condition of life: '*Light is sweet, and it pleases the eyes to see the sun.*' (Eccles. 11:7). Death and the fear of death had a role in Jesus' own experience (Heb. 5:7), and death is constantly described as the last enemy (1 Cor. 15).

This, then, is the first truth, the first fence of the enclosure that protects Christian hope: evil, as Henri Blocher summarises, is *totally*, *radically* and *absolutely* wicked.

The sovereignty of God

The conviction that the God of the Bible is the sovereign Lord comes directly from His revelation as creator, and is not something acquired through human investigation (Heb. 11:3).

> You are worthy, our Lord and God, to receive glory and honour and power, for you created all things, and by your will they were created and have their being (Rev. 4:11).

The authors of the Bible, expressing themselves in every register of language and literary form, never fail to underline this reality. There is nothing that escapes God's sovereignty (Isa. 45:9).[10] Theologians also talk

---

10   John Piper, *Coronavirus and Christ* (Crossway, 2020), pp. 37ff.

about 'providence', the way by which God sustains the world (Col. 1:17; Heb. 1:3). The traditional terms which are used to describe this attribute of God present us with the idea of divine government which is 'certain' but also rich and all-encompassing. Take, for example, the extraordinary revelation of Matthew 5:45: 'He causes his sun to rise on the evil and the good, and sends rain on the righteous and the unrighteous'.

The God of the Bible is sovereign because He is the creator! The fact that this creation is *ex nihilo* (from nothing) strengthens this notion: He is sovereign over every aspect and every element of reality, both static and dynamic (including human history itself, as we see in Acts 17:26). These statements, when they are considered within the tapestry of the Biblical narrative and the reflections of its authors, are qualified by many caveats. When they are taken out of this tapestry, this big picture, they must be handled with care, so as not to fall into determinism, or to give a helping hand to the powerful objections of atheism.[11] We don't have space here to expand upon the themes that flow from this clear affirmation of the Bible, but shortly we will discuss

11   See for example, John Lennox, *Determined to Believe: the Sovereignty of God, Freedom, Faith and Human Responsibility* (Oxford: Lion Hudson, 2017).

the questions which arise from this truth in relation to the spread of the epidemic.

So then, on the basis of the Biblical testimony, we may also affirm that God is *totally*, *radically* and *absolutely* sovereign.

The goodness of God

In his book, *How Long, O Lord?*, Don Carson affirms:

> If you work through the biblical passages that bluntly insist God in some sense stands behind evil, and do not simultaneously call to mind the countless passages that insist he is unfailingly good, then in a period of suffering you may be tempted to think of God as a vicious, sovereign thug.[12]

This appeal introduces us to the third biblical truth, the goodness of God. This truth also begins with creation and, in particular, the interpretation that God Himself gave to His own creative acts: 'God saw that it was [very] good' (Gen. 1:10, 12, 18, 21, 25, 31). And in this case as well, any investigation of the phenomena in our world would agree: many aspects of reality convey to us a sense of beauty, harmony, and goodness. But if the created reality is good, contrary to what dualistic or Manichean systems would have us believe (1 Tim. 4:4), this comes from the very nature of God Himself who is *good*.

---

12   D. A. Carson, *How Long, O Lord*, p. 225.

This is represented by the symbolism of light, as John declares: '*God is light; in him there is no darkness at all*' (1 John 1:5). And the mere possibility that God could encourage evil is excluded: God *cannot* tempt anyone (James 1:13). Goodness emanates from the symphony and harmony of all His attributes (Deut. 32:4, 'does no wrong') and the goodness of God is also declared by Jesus (Mark 10:18). And when the biblical God, in the fullness of His personhood, is confronted with the goodness of His world disfigured by man's disobedience (Rom. 8), we can sense the divine distress: 'Your eyes are too pure to look on evil…' (Hab. 1:13); 'For I take no pleasure in the death of anyone, declares the Sovereign Lord' (Ezek. 18:32).[13]

God is *totally*, *radically*, and *absolutely* good! This is the third fence, and we now have the three elements for the construction of the secure enclosure for Christian hope.

Some ambiguities

There are some obstacles, however. Many passages show that God is never surprised by manifestations of evil and of suffering (Gen. 50:19). Others show that He permits events which we would consider to be evil (Job

---

13 Jonathan Lamb, *From Why to Worship: an Introduction to the Book of Habakkuk*, (Carlisle: Langham Preaching Resources, 2018).

1:12, 2:6). There are still others which show that He is active in managing the flow of events which are clearly negative for humankind ('I form the light and create darkness, I bring prosperity and create disaster; I, the LORD, do all these things.' Isa. 45:7). And finally, in a surprising escalation, there is the theme of God's justice: His justice responds to the moral evil in the world (to 'sin') in ways that might also appear 'evil': death upon all men (Rom. 6:23).

In many of these passages it is the faith of the believer which speaks out and declares these truths (Job, Ruth, Jesus Himself); and there are also 'revealing' passages in which God Himself explains His actions in these terms: many of them are prophetic texts in which God opposes false gods. In confessing this truth we are confronted with the limitations of human language and understanding.

Our interlocutors to whom we wish to present Christian hope await us at the crossroad!

The present pandemic through which we are living – itself an event which does not fall outside divine sovereignty – compels us to ask: has it been sent directly by God for some precise reason or reasons which we are able to identify?[14] Or is the pandemic part of a general

---

14   John Piper, in his inspiring reflection on our experience, in *Coronavirus and Christ*, affirms: 'The coronavirus was sent,

picture in which, although we can affirm that it does not fall outside of God's sovereignty, it is to be attributed to secondary causes?[15]

Maintaining scriptural language here is vitally important: it is our guarantee. The Bible affirms that life and death are in God's hands. In the Biblical narrative we also find cases in which there is a special relationship which is mysteriously established between an event and the will of God (such as Paul's sinister pronouncement on the community of Corinth). But the Bible does not expect us, after we have confessed the Lord's sovereignty, to pursue at any cost a connection between a certain event, like the pandemic, and a certain way in which God is acting. We would all love to be able to see this connection; maybe one day we will have a general idea. To say, therefore, that this pandemic was willed by God for this or that reason is a language that does not

---

therefore, by God. This is not a season for sentimental views of God. It is a bitter season. And God ordained it. God governs it. He will end it. No part of it is outside his sway. Life and death are in his hand' (p. 42). In chapter 6, he says that God is 'Picturing Moral Horror'.

15 For example, in the movie *Contagion* (2011), by Steven Soderbergh, we see that a pandemic very similar to coronavirus (apart from cinematographic exaggeration) starts by reason of the deforestation of some of China's territory, with bats forced to move to where humans live, thereby infecting them.

seem to respect either the Biblical equilibrium, or the pain of the victims.

And here, perhaps I might be permitted to make a personal comment: alright, *you* speak with the family of the elderly who died in the rest homes in Lombardy, and *you* tell them that the coronavirus was sent by God to expose the wickedness in the world. My brother-in-law had been fighting a tumour for a year and a half; he was admitted to Parma Hospital just before the pandemic exploded; he needed treatment. He was mowed down by the virus in seven days. He was only 59. He died alone, vanishing from his loved ones' future. It is difficult for me, while blessing the name of the Lord, to believe that God willed my brother-in-law's death in order to display the moral corruption in our society. Maybe! I don't know; and because I don't know, it is best to be wary and to only go as far as to confess the three truths that I believe!

On the other hand, we need to remember the cautions which the Bible presents to us when we handle such themes. Three episodes from the Bible are enlightening, providing us with a general principle that invites us to *confess*, not to *reconcile*. This Biblical equilibrium is also an important guarantee for those to whom we appeal to embrace Christian hope.

Job's friends were sure that he was suffering because he had, most definitely, sinned; but this theory is refuted by the initial revelation of the heavenly mystery (the challenge between God and Satan – information which we do not have for the coronavirus); and the same theory is directly contested by the outcome of the theophany of God (Job 11:7). Then in the second episode – the man born blind in John 9 – it is Jesus Himself who rejects the insinuations of those involved about who is responsible for the man's disability. Finally, we can say, together with the Teacher in this third episode (Luke 13:1-5), that when we are confronted with a tragedy – the fall of a tower or Herod's insane murder – it should stimulate solidarity and encourage repentance.

The attempt to perfectly explain the three truths is complicated and dangerous. John Lennox admits: 'experience shows us that none of us has ever been satisfied with the solution to this particular argument'.[16]

When it comes to reconciling the sovereignty and goodness of God with the reality and negativity of evil, we are inevitably dissatisfied with the best solutions proposed by human thought. Some philosophers have defined these solutions as 'strategies of immunization' for the conscience towards evil. Henri Blocher groups these strategies into the three categories of *optimism*,

---

16   John Lennox, *Where is God in a Coronavirus World*, p. 42.

dualism, and *pessimism*. We will let him respond to these various strategies:

> If beneath the outward appearance of the evil there were hidden something good, why would anyone want to see it disappear? [*against* optimism] If God were not sovereign, how would he bring under his control what is not dependent on him? [*against* dualism] If God concealed darkness within himself, how would it not be eternal, like him? [*against* pessimism]
>
> But 'God's solid foundation stands firm' (2 Tim. 2:19). When wild hopes disappear into thin air, the foundation of hope comes into view, the sovereignty of the God who fights against evil, and who invites us to join him in the battle.[17]

Once our three truths are believed and confessed – all the while admitting the difficulty in reconciling them – they actually define a space, an enclosure, in which hope can live and grow, protected by these convictions, even if it is 'hope against hope' (Rom. 4:18). This possibility becomes more concrete when you look at the essential reason why we cannot find a definitive solution to the problem of evil. To understand its essence would be to consider evil an element of the created reality; it is indeed this reality which we as beings created in the image of God must investigate, explain and understand.

---

17   Henri Blocher, *Evil and the Cross*, p. 103.

We have understood and explained many aspects of reality, and in the end we may also come to understand the coronavirus. To confess the three truths does not put us in the agnostic corner; rather it places us in the centre of the ring in which we can fight evil – exactly what the God of the Bible has been doing since the beginning!

Whoever does not believe is invited to consider this possibility.

Hope within a secure enclosure

Hope grappling with the wicked and negative reality of evil

The public official from Piacenza whom we quoted at the beginning affirmed: 'Everything that we salvage will be *a timid and trembling hope,* suspended amongst the heap of ruins' (L. Civardi). The spread of the coronavirus is capable of devastating lives and isolating people (despite the hashtag *#uniticelafaremo,* 'united we can do it').[18] Holding steady the two truths of the sovereignty and goodness of God, we can affirm that when Christian hope is confronted with all this, several things are discovered.

---

18   L. Civardi: 'It is not easy when we discover that others cannot comfort us because they experience the same disquiet that we do, that every phone call with friends is focused on foggy predictions of a future maybe more terrifying than the present.'

We discover lament: *Christian hope is a hope that laments.* Confronted with the image of the coffins transported by army trucks in Bergamo, the Christian discovers that lament is a means to draw close to God – with whom else could we lament? – to protest, to wrestle with God, bringing before Him the horror that we are experiencing.[19] How could we not mention here the example of Habakkuk:

> How long, LORD, must I call for help, but you do not listen? Or cry out to you, 'Violence!' but you do not save? Why do you make me look at injustice? Why do you tolerate wrongdoing? Destruction and violence are before me; there is strife, and conflict abounds (Hab. 1:2-3).

Christian hope is an empathetic hope. Second, the hope which comes from suffering is able to perceive the suffering of others as well as to identify with those who suffer. Jesus in Gethsemane asks for a similar empathy from His disciples, but does not receive it … He finds them sleeping in the hour of His anguish. By contrast, the teacher of Ecclesiastes reminds us that:

> The day of death (is) better than the day of birth. It is better to go to a house of mourning than to go to a house of feasting, for death is the destiny of everyone; the living should take this to heart.

19   Pablo Martinez, *A Thorn in the Flesh*, p. 35.

> Frustration is better than laughter, because a sad face is good for the heart. The heart of the wise is in the house of mourning, but the heart of fools is in the house of pleasure (Eccles. 7:1-4).

Nicholas Wolterstorff, in his greatest written work after the death of his son, asks believers not to speak, not to judge, but because of their safeguarded hope, simply to sit alongside those who are suffering on their *bench of grief*:

> What I need to hear from you is that you recognize how painful it is. I need to hear from you that you are with me in my desperation. To comfort me, you have to come close. Come sit beside me on my mourning bench.[20]

Thirdly, *Christian hope is a hope that takes a stand.* The hope that is made secure within the enclosure of these three truths is conscious of evil's wickedness, and takes responsibility in not giving concessions to evil and to suffering. It moves in favour of justice and good, sometimes desperately, but always with the conviction that evil and suffering cannot be ignored and must be confronted. This is expressed well in point 5 of the Lausanne Covenant:

---

20   Nicholas Wolterstorff, *Lament for a Son* (London: SPCK, 1997), p. 34.

The message of salvation implies also a message of judgment upon every form of alienation, oppression and discrimination, and we should not be afraid to denounce evil and injustice wherever they exist. When people receive Christ they are born again into his kingdom and must seek not only to exhibit but also to spread its righteousness in the midst of an unrighteous world. The salvation we claim should be transforming us in the totality of our personal and social responsibilities. Faith without works is dead.[21]

Hope grappling with the Sovereignty of God

Christian hope trusts in the fact that God is sovereign (Ps. 39:7). For 12 years, without explanation, we were without children: never as at that time did we feel that He who holds the fate of nature and the cycle of life in His hand, as the Bible teaches, was encamped around us. We were made the object of His attention, but in a contrary way: infertility. We experienced a suffering faith; we tried not to forget that God is good and is not stained by any collusion with evil; we found new faces to hope!

Christian hope drives us to worship

I give credit to the Psalms that exalt the King of all the earth for the privilege of having understood this truth,

---

21 See John Stott, *For the Lord We Love: Your Study Guide to The Lausanne Covenant*, The Didasko Files, 2009, p. 28.

even in the midst of difficulty. The faithful believer indeed blesses the name of God even in adversity, though maybe with tears in his eyes. It is praise, the shout of jubilee, that will be strongest in the moments in which the omnipotence of God is manifest, made evident in a deliverance, in the answer to prayer. And this praise will exclaim 'Your kingdom come' (Ps. 146:5; Jer. 29:11; Matt. 6:10).

Christian hope implores

Along with praise, the hope which looks at and confesses God's sovereignty also has the courage to lift up supplications to Him for healing, for deliverance, just like the extreme prayer of Jesus in Gethsemane, which in the end surrenders to the will of the Father. This request for deliverance is pressing and insistent (just as Paul repeatedly prayed about the thorn), because evil hurts and God's sovereignty 'can guarantee the order in view of which evil is denounced as disorder'.

Christian hope is committed to perseverance and sanctification

This is an unexpected turn from hope. It arises from the perspective on the future which God's sovereignty provides us, about which Jonathan Lamb has written in the previous chapter. This way to live out our hope is in direct contrast to the moral version of evil:

> Dear friends, now we are children of God, and what
> we will be has not yet been made known. But we
> know that when Christ appears, we shall be like
> him, for we shall see him as he is. All who have this
> hope in him purify themselves, just as he is pure
> (1 John 3:2-3).

Maybe we can personally own the suggestion of some
theologians by considering God's sovereignty a relational
attribute, a way in which the God of the Bible leads this
world, asking those who boast of knowing Him to walk
this road together with Him: in prayer, in whisper, and in
dialogue.

Hope grappling with the goodness of God

Remembering God's sovereignty, together with the
wickedness of evil, we come to the third truth. God's
goodness reveals to us further significant dimensions
of Christian hope. God's goodness is the root of all that
is good which exists in reality (Phil. 4:8). The distortions
of evil, of tragedies and of wickedness, only stimulate
Christian hope to reach towards the final horizon.

Christian hope intercedes for others, for their good;
for blessing, not cursing. Amidst tragedy, when anguish
and panic assail men's hearts, Christians have always
distinguished themselves in their commitment to the
good of others, first of all in prayer. In how many prayer
meetings during this pandemic have the Christians of

the world prayed for those who are ill, for those dying and for the families of those who are dying; for health workers, for the authorities!

Christian hope moves to action, to seek actively the good of the city (Jer. 29:7). In Italy, in the worst of the pandemic, the initiatives undertaken by Christians (in a broad sense) to try to help alleviate suffering are too many to count. Even the commitment with which the quarantine was lived out has something 'Christian' about it. There wasn't just the defence of 'naked life', as the philosopher Agamben maintains; care for one's neighbour played its role, a care which Luther had expressed well in his letter about the epidemic of 1527:

> What else is the epidemic but a fire which instead of consuming wood and straw devours life and body? You ought to think this way: Very well, by God's decree the enemy has sent us poison and deadly garbage. Therefore, I will ask God mercifully to protect us. Then I will disinfect, help purify the air, give and take medicine. I will avoid places and persons where my presence is not needed in order not to become contaminated and thus perhaps infect and transmit it to others, and so cause their death as a result of my negligence.[22]

---

22 Martin Luther, 'Whether One May Flee From A Deadly Plague', https://blogs.lcms.org/wp-content/uploads/2020/03/Plague-blogLW.pdf

The cross

But the utmost resource for Christian hope, that which is seen when remaining firmly planted in the enclosure of the three biblical truths, is represented by a precise point in history: by the cross on which Jesus was hung and died two thousand years ago. Isaac Watts, the 18th century hymn writer, named one of his compositions, *When I survey the wondrous cross*, and this title states exactly the position which men and women must adopt. We must do so even – especially – when we are wrestling with such an insidious manifestation of natural evil, the coronavirus pandemic. It is at the cross where the three truths that we have examined become intertwined, blending one into another into the greatest mystery of human history.

We are struck by the physical pain of the cross, which permits us to see the suffering that only faith can discern: the spiritual suffering of Him who was 'made sin for us'.

At the cross we see how God's sovereignty subverts the plans of men, such that the immeasurable pride of man, thinking to satisfy his own aims, could do no other than fulfil God's plans (Acts 4:27-8).

The cross is the quintessential act of love and goodness:

At the cross, who would dare entertain the blasphemy of imagining that God would, even to the slightest degree, comply with evil? It brought him death, in the person of his Son. Holiness stands revealed. Love stands revealed, a pure love; there is no love greater. Because of the cross we shall praise his goodness, the goodness of his justice, the goodness of his grace, through all eternity. At the cross, God turned evil against evil and brought about the practical solution to the problem. He has made atonement for sin, he has conquered death, he has triumphed over the devil. He has laid the foundation for hope.[23]

When hope stays within the enclosure constructed by these three truths, it is truly living and active. The three truths, focussed in the event of the cross, guarantee an acceptable and reasonable vision of hope which we then offer to those who do not yet believe.

Confessing the wickedness of evil, we do justice to the victims of any tragedy.

Confessing the sovereignty of God, we proclaim the final victory of the Lord.

Confessing the goodness of God, we avoid falling into fatalism and experience His care.

---

23   Henri Blocher, *Evil and the Cross*, p. 104.

Epilogue

How to Discover, Live and Protect the Christian Hope

Question: *What is your only comfort in life and death?*

Answer:

That I am not my own,

> **1 Corinthians 6:19-20 ESV** Or do you not know that your body is a temple of the Holy Spirit within you, whom you have from God? You are not your own, for you were bought with a price. So glorify God in your body.

but belong with body and soul, both in life and in death,

> **Romans 14:7-9 ESV** For none of us lives to himself, and none of us dies to himself. For if we live, we live to the Lord, and if we die, we die to the Lord. So then, whether we live or whether we die, we are the

Lord's. For to this end Christ died and lived again, that he might be Lord both of the dead and of the living.

to my faithful Saviour Jesus Christ

1 Corinthians 3:23 ESV and you are Christ's, and Christ is God's.

He has fully paid for all my sins

1 John 1:7 ESV ... and the blood of Jesus his Son cleanses us from all sin.

with His precious blood,

1 Peter 1:18-19 ESV knowing that you were ransomed from the futile ways inherited from your forefathers, not with perishable things such as silver or gold, but with the precious blood of Christ, like that of a lamb without blemish or spot.

and has set me free from all the power of the devil.

Hebrews 2:14-15 ESV Since therefore the children share in flesh and blood, he himself likewise partook of the same things, that through death he might destroy the one who has the power of death, that is, the devil, and deliver all those who through fear of death were subject to lifelong slavery.

He also preserves me in such a way

> **John 6:39 ESV** And this is the will of him who sent me, that I should lose nothing of all that he has given me, but raise it up on the last day.

that without the will of my heavenly Father not a hair can fall from my head;

> **Matthew 10:30 ESV** But even the hairs of your head are all numbered.

indeed, all things must work together for my salvation.

> **Romans 8:28 ESV** And we know that for those who love God all things work together for good, for those who are called according to his purpose.

Therefore, by His Holy Spirit He also assures me of eternal life

> **2 Corinthians 1:22 ESV** and who has also put his seal on us and given us his Spirit in our hearts as a guarantee.

and makes me heartily willing and ready from now on to live for Him

> **Romans 8:14 ESV** For all who are led by the Spirit of God are sons of God.

A prayer adapted from the catechism

What is your only comfort in life and death?

Heavenly Father,

I acknowledge that I am not my own, but belong both body and soul, and in life and in death, to my faithful Saviour Jesus Christ.

I believe that He has fully paid for all my sins with His precious blood, and has set me free from all the power of the devil.

I thank you that He also preserves me in such a way that without the will of my heavenly Father not a hair can fall from my head; indeed, thank you that all things must work together for my salvation.

Therefore, I ask that by your Holy Spirit you also assure me of eternal life and make me heartily willing and ready from now on to live for you.

Amen.

A CHRISTIAN'S POCKET GUIDE TO

SUFFERING

BRIAN H. COSBY

How God Shapes Us through Pain and Tragedy

A Christian's Pocket Guide to Suffering

How God Shapes Us through Pain and Tragedy

Brian H. Cosby

When tragedy strikes-the death of a child, hurricanes, a school shooting-we begin looking for an escape from the pain, a way out, or we clamor for answers from a panel of religious 'experts' to explain the ever-present question, 'Why?' We want answers and we want to believe that our suffering isn't meaningless.

A Christian's Pocket Guide to Suffering seeks to simply, but clearly, present a biblical view of suffering so that your feet might land on the solid foundation of God's Word and the God of that Word and, there, find understanding and hope. All other ground is sinking sand.

If you find yourself wandering in the valley of the shadow of death and see no signs to show you the way through, pick up this little book and read it! It offers sound, Christ-centered, biblical, and yet eminently practical counsel on suffering.

J. V. Fesko
Academic Dean and Professor of Systematic and Historical Theology, Westminster Seminary, Escondido, California

Christian Focus Publications

Our mission statement —

STAYING FAITHFUL

In dependence upon God we seek to impact the world through literature faithful to His infallible Word, the Bible. Our aim is to ensure that the Lord Jesus Christ is presented as the only hope to obtain forgiveness of sin, live a useful life and look forward to heaven with Him.

Our books are published in four imprints:

CHRISTIAN FOCUS

Popular works including biographies, commentaries, basic doctrine and Christian living.

CHRISTIAN HERITAGE

Books representing some of the best material from the rich heritage of the church.

MENTOR

Books written at a level suitable for Bible College and seminary students, pastors, and other serious readers. The imprint includes commentaries, doctrinal studies, examination of current issues and church history.

CF4·K

Children's books for quality Bible teaching and for all age groups: Sunday school curriculum, puzzle and activity books; personal and family devotional titles, biographies and inspirational stories — because you are never too young to know Jesus!

Christian Focus Publications Ltd,
Geanies House, Fearn, Ross-shire,
IV20 1TW, Scotland, United Kingdom.
www.christianfocus.com